I. INTRODUCTION

In the early 1980's, President Ronald Reagan suggested a mutual security arrangement between Brazil and the United States.[1] The idea was never acted upon due to Brazilian disinterest. This thesis will analyze the plausibility of such an arrangement in today's international system with regard to a regional maritime defense of the South Atlantic. In order to do so, the changing global community and nature of security alliances must first be examined.

Of primary importance is an accurate assessment of threat to the region. To some, revelations of a Soviet economy with zero or even negative growth in 1990, claims of sovereignty by fourteen of the fifteen republics, Gorbachev's declining popularity at home, low morale and poor living conditions all appear to give credence to the argument that the United States can afford to disarm and enjoy a "peace dividend."

There are loud voices in the U.S. Congress calling for huge defense budget cuts, and the effects of these are already being felt. Indeed, the international system is changing and for the time being, East-West frictions appear to be at their lowest level since World War II. This, however, does not necessarily mean that the United States can demobilize. Other problems in the world system are gaining increasing prominence. Terrorism, narco-trafficking, the

---

[1]*Brazil: A Country Study*, United States Government as represented by the Secretary of the Army, 1983, p. 282.

spread of high technology conventional and nuclear weapons to the developing world, and the rise of ethnic tensions worldwide are filling any gap that the declining Soviet threat may have created. The recent Iraqi invasion of Kuwait and concomitant United States response serve to underscore the endless volatility in the Middle East. And despite the perception of a decreased Soviet threat, the Soviet Union continues to modernize its armed forces, to engage in international intelligence gathering, to support regimes hostile to the United States, and is still the most potent threat to the existence of the United States, even without its Warsaw Pact allies.[2]

Some have suggested that the United States' widening defense resource gap could be filled by increased burden sharing of its allies.[3] Would a cutback in the U.S. Navy's budget prevent adequate coverage of the South Atlantic in time of war, and if so, could this coverage be assumed or augmented by a capable ally such as Brazil?

Political Scientist Philip Kelly made the following comment in his book, *Geopolitics of the Southern Cone and Antarctica*:

> From a geopolitical standpoint, it is surprising that the United States does not forge closer strategic linkages with Brazil. The two nations are natural allies in the sense that their spheres of influence do not overlap, they share similar foreign policy traditions (neither condone extracontinental intrusions into America that might destabilize frontiers), they occupy continental

---

[2]Admiral Carlisle A. H. Trost USN, "Maritime Strategy for the 1990's", *U.S. Naval Institute Proceedings*, May 1990, p. 98.
[3]Among them, President Bush in the 1990 *National Security Strategy of the United States*. p. 3.

locations peripheral to Eurasia, and their diplomatic heritages are American, Western, pacific and commercial.[4]

A. WHY A NAVAL PARTNERSHIP, AND WHY WITH BRAZIL?

What exactly is meant by the term "naval partnership," and why a naval partnership instead of a full blown joint military alliance or some other type of mutual security arrangement with Brazil?   The following definitions are provided in order to better understand the nature of international partnerships:

•Alliances--multilateral agreements between two or more states made to improve their power position for the purpose of defending common interests.[5]   Treaties are written to formalize alliances, however not all alliances are spelled out in treaties. Some alliances are forged under the aegis of executive agreements.

•Treaties--formal agreements entered into between two or more states for the purpose of defining or limiting mutual rights and responsibilities.[6]   Treaties must be approved by two thirds vote in the Senate, and require Presidential ratification.

•Executive agreements--international agreements between the President of the United States and foreign heads of state. Executive agreements are less formal than treaties and do not require Senate consent.[7]

Alliances are formed either for economic reasons (as in the case of the Organization of Petroleum Exporting Countries [OPEC]), or for

---

[4]Philip Kelly and Jack Child, eds. *Geopolitics of the Southern Cone and Antarctica* (Boulder and London: Lynne Rienner Publishers, 1988), p. 114.
[5]Jack Plano, Milton Greenberg, *The American Political Dictionary*, (Hinsdale: The Dryden Press, 1979), p. 379.
[6]Plano and Greenberg, *The American Political Dictionary*, p. 410.
[7]Plano and Greenberg, *The American Political Dictionary*, p. 389.

national security reasons (as in the case of the North Atlantic Treaty Organization [NATO]). National security alliances will henceforth be referred to as military alliances. The following definitions are useful when discussing military alliances:

•Combined operations--military operations in which U.S. forces act in concert with foreign allied forces (also called force integration).[8]

•Joint operations--military operations in which U.S. air, land and naval forces act in concert with one another.[9]

The term "naval partnership" as it is used here refers to a military alliance between the United states and Brazil, involving force integration between the navies of each country. This naval partnership is not "joint" in the traditional sense because it involves only the navies of each country (and the maritime component of the Brazilian air force). The navy was chosen because as a maritime nation, much of Brazil's national and economic security hinges on its ability to maintain open sea lines of communication. It is for this reason that Brazil currently possesses a nav. 'that is ranked among the top three in the third world based on capability.[10] Similarly, the United States, as a two-ocean nation is dependent on a strong navy to

[8]Chief of Naval Operations, *The Maritime Strategy*, OPNAV 60 P-i-8y, Department of the Navy, Revision 4, 23 February 1989, pp. 8, 19.
[9]Chief of Naval Operations, *The Maritime Strategy*, OPNAV 60 P-1-89, Department of the Navy, Revision 4, 23 February 1989, pp. 8, 19.
[10]Michael A. Morris, *Expansion of Third World Navies*, (London: MacMillan Press, 1987), pp. 25, 26.

protect its overseas interests as well as to ensure freedom of the seas for its commerce and to promote the free passage of strategic raw materials. The two countries have similar needs in this regard, although the United States as a superpower has maritime interests of a much larger scope.

There are other factors which make Brazil a logical choice for a naval partner. Brazil was the only Latin American country to declare war on the Central powers in World War I, and it fought alongside the United States in World War II. In addition, the Brazilian arms industry has been among the largest in the third world, giving Brazil some capability to modernize forces with its own military industrial complex.

A naval partnership between the two countries could be mutually beneficial, not only for present security considerations, but for other reasons as well. The enhanced power status and prestige accorded to Brazil from working closely with a recognized world power could create an atmosphere of respect and cooperation leading to the following positive developments for both countries:

•A partnership formulated and strengthened now could be useful in the event of a future threat to the Western hemisphere, or provide a basis for future Brazilian military support in crises such as the 1990-1991 Middle East crisis.

•A defensive partnership could promote better relations between the two countries and provide some common ground in cooperative experience which is presently missing. A partnership could give the United States a bigger "foot in the door" to better

5

address and cooperate on problems such as narco-terrorism, debt reduction, and environmental concerns.

•A partnership could be seen by neighboring countries as a positive North/South development which would serve to diffuse the "anti-Yankeeism" attitudes of many Latin Americans.

B. FORMULA FOR VIABLE ALLIANCE: A HYPOTHESIS TESTING MATRIX

Before a naval partnership can be considered, the determinants of a viable alliance must first be investigated. K. J. Holsti asser that military alliances can be classified and compared according to the nature of the casus foederis (the catalyst for action), the type of action to be taken in the event of this catalyst, whether or not combined operations are to be used, and the geographical scope of the alliance.[11]

Holsti goes on to describe four sources of conflict which may arise among the members of an alliance and may weaken its viability. These include the development of diverging objectives, the development of a threat against only one or a few of the partners within the alliance, incompatibility of social and political values, and the development of nuclear weapons by one or more members of the alliance.[12]

These terms are explained below:[13]

---

[11]K. J. Holsti, *International Politics, A Framework for Analysis*, (Englewood Cliffs: Prentice Hall, 1988) pp. 103-107.
[12]Holsti, *International Politics, A Framework for Analysis*, pp. 107--110.
[13]Explanation of terms from Holsti, pp. 103--107.

1. Casus Foederis

The casus foederis is the catalyst required for mutual commitments to become operational. Usually, the more precisely the casus foederis is defined, the more viable the alliance is, however this is not always the case. An example of a treaty with a vague casus foederis is the 1939 German-Italian "Pact of Steel" which stated:

> If it should happen, against the wishes and hopes of the contracting parties, that one of them should become involved in warlike complications . . . the other contracting party will come to its aid as an ally and will support it with all its military forces.[14]

The wording "warlike complications" was so vague and general that Italy was committed to assist Hitler in almost any situation. A vaguely worded casus foederis is often times characteristic of an offensive alliance as opposed to a defensive one.

In a defensive alliance, a vague casus foederis could allow signatories to apply a wide range of interpretation on whether or not the "catalyst" was actually taking place. It is for this reason that a precisely worded casus foederis, where there is little room for interpretation, is characteristic of a more viable treaty. An example of a treaty with a precisely worded casus foederis is the North Atlantic Treaty Organization (NATO) treaty which states:

---

[14]Holsti, *International Politics, A Framework for Analysis*, p. 104.

...an armed attack on one or more of the parties is deemed to include an attack on the territory of any of the Parties.[15]

2. Commitment of Signatories

Similar to the casus foederis, the commitment required of signatories can either be written in vague or precise language. A precisely defined commitment may, for example, call for "immediate military counterattack" in the event of attack. This type of response is also referred to as a "hair trigger" clause. With a hair trigger clause, there is no room and no time for policy makers to discuss possible alternative courses of action once the casus foederis occurs. An example of a vaguely written commitment clause would call an ally to "act against the danger" in the event of the casus foederis. This wording is so vague that there are a myriad of options and interpretations with no precise time element in which to implement them. The more precisely worded commitment is characteristic of a more viable treaty.

3. Integration of Forces

Integration of forces is rare in most alliances. It entails one or more of the following actions:

- establishing a supreme commander over all allied forces;
- standardizing weapons systems;
- integrating personnel of different countries into one command structure; and
- permitting one of the partners to draft and direct war plans for the alliance.[16]

---

[15] Holsti, *International Politics, A Framework for Analysis*, p. 106.
[16] Holsti, *International Politics, A Framework for Analysis*, p. 105.

Alliances that have planned force integration are more flexible and better trained (out of necessity) than those that do not.

4. Geographical Scope

Geographical scope is usually precisely defined in alliances. The most common consideration is whether or not to include overseas colonies or territorial possessions of the signatories.

5. Diverging Objectives

The development of diverging objectives with regard to political, social, economic or military issues between signatories of an alliance can cause strains. For example, Pakistan joined the SEATO (Southeast Asia Collective Defense Treaty) alliance not primarily to oppose China or Russia as Washington had hoped, but instead to get access to sophisticated weaponry with which to counter India.

Those alliances in which the signatories either have no diverging objectives, or can down play the importance of their diverging objectives by concentrating on objectives of higher importance are the most viable alliances.

6. Similar Threat Perception

The most critical characteristic of a viable alliance is common threat perception. It can "paper over" alliance strains in other areas or lead to a total breakdown in an alliance if not present. Post 1990 NATO is undergoing a transitional period where an ill-defined threat is currently calling the utility of the alliance into question.

7. Compatibility of Major Social and Political Values

Examples of major social and political values contrasted include:

• Capitalism vs. Communism
• Sunni vs. Shiite
• Democracy vs. Dictatorship

As long as nation states face a common enemy, ideological incompatibilities seldom prevent the formation of alliances. Nation states of homogeneous ideologies however are more likely to be more committed to the alliance.

8. Development of Nuclear weapons

This variable may cause either a strain in an alliance or strengthen it depending on the relationship between the United States and the nuclear capable country. In the case of NATO, Britain's possession of nuclear weapons causes no problem, but France's nuclear capability does. Nuclear capability of a third world alliance partner would most likely cause a strain in the alliance given the U.S. stance on non-proliferation.

The major United States treaties in place at present include NATO (North Atlantic Treaty Organization), ANZUS (Australia, New Zealand, United States), SEATO (Southeast Asia Collective Defense Treaty), and the IATRA (Inter-American Treaty of Reciprocal Assistance or Rio Treaty). Before we discuss the viability of a bilateral U.S./Brazilian alliance, we will analyze the viability of the North Atlantic Treaty Organization. Then, we will examine the

Organization of American States, and the Inter-American Treaty of Reciprocal Assistance, (the IATRA or Rio Treaty), two institutions currently in place which were constructed for the purpose of hemispheric defense.

As the first effective North American military alliance since the early 1800's, and the United States' most important and elaborate defense commitment,[17] the pre-1990 NATO alliance provides a useful standard by which the viability of all alliances can be measured. Not surprisingly, the pre-1990 NATO alliance positively correlates to all of Holsti's comparative categories.

There have been rifts in the treaty such as France's secession from military involvement, the unequal burdensharing debate, and the problems with internal rivalry such as that experienced by Greece and Turkey. Notwithstanding, the alliance has held together and remained viable for over forty years. Its expressed purpose was to prevent the spread of communism past the Eastern Bloc into Western Europe, and it achieved this. The Treaty actually did more than achieve this as demonstrated by the crumbling of the Communist Bloc and the now dubious utility of the Warsaw Pact to the Soviet Union. Moscow's initial concern with the balance of power shift following the reunification of Germany gives further proof that the Soviets *perceived* NATO as a threat. By anyone's standard, the NATO alliance would have to be considered a successful strategy for

---

[17]Terry L. Deibel, *Changing Patterns of Collective Defense: U.S. Security Commitments in the Third World*, in Alan Ned Sabrosky, ed. *Alliances in U.S. Foreign Policy*, (Boulder and London: Westview Press, 1988), p. 107.

its time. The current viability of the NATO alliance has recently been called into question following events in the Soviet Union and Eastern Bloc, so we will only be concerned with the pre-1990 portion of the NATO alliance.

The NATO alliance can be analyzed using Holsti's eight criteria as follows:

•Is the Casus Foederis (Catalyst for Action) specified?

Yes. Military measures can only be taken in responses to armed attack on one of the signatories.

•Is the type of action to be taken by signatories specified?

Yes. Every signatory is required to come to the aid of the attacked state.

•Are plans in place to use integrated forces?

Yes, with a Supreme Commander over all forces provided by the United States.

•Is there a specific geographical Scope?

Yes. Article five of the treaty states "...an armed attack on one or more of the Parties is deemed to include an attack on the territory of any of the Parties . . ."

•Are alliance members free of diverging objectives?

Yes. All signatories recognize the need for a common defense against Soviet encroachment. There are minor divergences, but recognition of this main purpose overshadows them.

•Is there a clear perception of threat with no collateral threat to one or a few allies?

Yes. Turkey and Greece created strains between themselves and other NATO members with the Cyprus conflict, but the clear perception of Soviet threat by all signatories has overshadowed incidents such as these.

•Is there compatibility of social and political values between the allies?

Generally yes. Turkey is the only non-Christian country in NATO.

•Do members other than the United States have nuclear weapons?

Yes, France and the United Kingdom do. U.S has expressed concern that French could use nuclear weapons in a manner contrary to U.S. interests. Washington assumes that France would automatically drag the United States into a war in which French nuclear weapons were used. France on the other hand has argued that Washington would be unwilling to use its nuclear weapons to support an ally because this could mean destruction of the United States by Soviet nuclear retaliation.

Holsti's eight criteria can be viewed as independent variables in a hypothesis testing matrix. The stated hypothesis in this model is:

"The degree of alliance viability is directly proportional to the number of independent variables that positively correlate."

In other words, those alliances to which a "yes" answer occurs in every block of the hypothesis testing matrix are more viable than those alliances for which less than every block of the matrix contains a "yes" answer. The hypothesis testing matrix is provided in Figure 1, on the following page.

⇨ INDEPENDENT VARIABLES ⇨   DEPEN-DENT VAR-IABLE ⇨

A	B	C	D	E	F	G	H	
Casus Foederis precise?	Commit-ment precise and auto-matic?	Force integra-tion?	Geo-graphical scope precise?	Free of Diverg-ing Objec-tives?	Clear threat percep-tion. No collat-eral threats?	Compat-bility of social and political values?	Members have Nuc Weaps?	
YES	YES	YES	YES	YES	YES	YES	YES	= Highly Viable Alliance

Figure 1:
Hypothesis Testing Matrix: NATO as a Test Case

The independent variables in this model do not possess the same degree of importance. Clear perception of threat (variable "F") possesses the most weight, and can influence the applicability of the other categories. For example, one could argue that the ANZUS Treaty (Australia, New Zealand, U.S.) was weakened by New Zealand's refusal to allow nuclear ships into its ports. This would seem to suggest that category "G", (compatibility of social and political values) was the "alliance buster". In a broader context, this argument could be repudiated by arguing that the United States and New Zealand do not share a similar perception of threat (Category "F"). If they did, U.S. nuclear powered ships would be welcomed in New Zealand.

Having established NATO as the standard by which to measure alliances using the criteria as set forth by Holsti, we are now in a position to evaluate the viability of other alliances or potential alliances.

II. HISTORICAL BACKGROUND

The United States has harbored the idea of Pan American defense since World War I. This idea has survived (at least on paper) to the present day as demonstrated by the maritime strategy of the United States Navy which suggests a cooperative maritime defense of southern oceans with Latin American navies.[18]

A. THE PAN AMERICAN MOVEMENT

The Pan American movement went through several phases of relationships throughout its history (see Figure 2 below).

---

[18]Chief of Naval Operations, *The Maritime Strategy*, OPNAV 60 P-1-89, Department of the Navy, Revision 4, 23 February 1989, p. 7.

The concept of Pan Americanism came into use in the 1880's and provided a point of departure from the unilateral Monroe Doctrine to the idea of a multilateral Inter-American concept. Institutionally, the Inter-American system began with the International Conference of American States which took place in Washington in 1889. The system developed in an ad-hoc manner over the next thirty five years. Several specialized agencies were created between 1902 and 1945 such as the Pan American Health Organization, the Inter-American Institute of Agricultural Sciences, and the Inter-American Defense Board.[19]

From 1945 to 1948 these institutions became more formalized and expanded. Both the Inter-American Treaty of Reciprocal Assistance (IATRA or Rio Treaty) and the Organization of American States (OAS) were established. Latin Americans were fully supportive of these developments, particularly after becoming fearful of waning United States interest in Inter-American Affairs due to Washington's enthusiasm for the newly organized United Nations. The Chapultapec Conference of 1945 was an effort to establish a formal juridical basis for the Inter-American System and paved the way for the Special Rio de Janeiro conference in 1947 which produced the Rio Treaty.[20]

---

[19]G. Pope Atkins, *Latin America in the International Political System*, (Boulder; Westview Press, 1989), p. 207.

[20]Atkins, *Latin America in the International Political System*, p. 207.

B. THE MUTUAL SECURITY IDEA

The mutual security idea developed into one of the main purposes of the Inter-American System. This required the development of mutual security arrangements which were first incorporated in 1938. They were redefined during World War II and then stated in the OAS charter and Rio Treaty. Some Inter-American security concepts dealt with outside threats, but most dealt with conflicts among the American States themselves.[21]

Prior to 1930, the United States considered the unilateral Monroe Doctrine the quintessential security concept for the hemisphere. In a departure from this position the United States attempted to mount a unified Pan American front against the Central powers during World War I, but Latin America failed to comply. Brazil was the only South American State to declare war.

Figure 3 describes the evolution of Pan American Security doctrine from a **policy making** viewpoint:

---

[21] Atkins, *Latin America in the International Political System*, p. 218.

Jack Child has argued that the United States and Latin America have been in an unequal military alliance since 1930 which has had two periods of growth and decline since its creation:

•creation and growth in World War II;
•divergence and decline in the early Cold War years (1945-1961);
•expansion and rebirth during the guerilla warfare period of the 1960's; and
•fragmentation and dysfunction in the contemporary years.[22]

Figure 4 (below) describes the evolution of Pan American Security doctrine from a **strategic** viewpoint:

---

[22]John Child, *Unequal Alliance; The Inter American Military System, 1938-1978*, (Boulder: Westview Press, 1980), p. 1.

There has been a wealth of planning and policy guidance concerning hemispheric defense. The culmination of this planning was the O.A.S (Organization of American States), and the Rio Treaty.

The Organization of American States was formed in 1948, and was concerned with formalizing rules and procedures within the western hemisphere such as:

- Settling regional disputes by peaceful means;
- Rendering mutual assistance in the event of external aggression;
- Stressing "representative democracy" to maintain the solidarity between States;
- The need for economic cooperation between states and upholding human rights.[23]

The OAS has been utilized several times in concert with the Rio Treaty but also by itself, most notably during the 1954 U.S. intervention into Guatemala, the 1962 Cuban missile crisis, and the 1981 armed conflict between Ecuador and Peru.[24] In more recent years however, the Organization of American States (OAS) has been used more as a political instrument to oppose the United States than as a basis for coalition defense. Members use it to suit their particular needs. It has been used to unify Latin American opinion against the United States (as was done during the Grenada and Panamanian invasions), and to gain support for a national cause (as Argentina attempted to do during its invasion of the Falklands).

---

[23]Harold Molineu, *U.S. Policy Toward Latin America*, (Westview Press: Boulder) 1986, pp. 27.
[24]Atkins *Latin America in the International Political System*, pp. 222, 223.

The OAS has not lived up to the expectations of its founders. From the Latin American perspective, the OAS has failed because the United States disregarded it on several occasions with regards to non-intervention. From the U.S. perspective, the OAS has demonstrated increasing impotence. The Latin American countries rejected the U.S. call for collective action by the OAS regarding intervention during the Nicaraguan revolution. In El Salvador, the OAS gave public support for democratic principles and elections, but declined to take an active role in seeing that they were implemented.[25] The OAS called for a diplomatic solution to the mounting friction between the United States and Panama between 1987 and 1989. The failure of these efforts led to U.S. military intervention in 1989.

Further evidence of the organization's declining importance is the Latin American formulation of the Contadora Group,[26] the Latin American Economic System (SELA), and the Esquipulus II accords,[27] all initiatives that would have been performed by the OAS had it been more viable.

The viability of the Rio Treaty for hemispheric defense will be discussed in the next chapter.

---

[25]Margaret Daly Hayes, *Latin America and the U.S. National Interest*, (Boulder: Westview Press, 1984), p. 250.

[26]Colombia, Mexico, Panama and Venezuela formed the Contadora group in 1983. The group proposed to serve as a mediator in seeking peaceful negotiation in Central America.

[27]President Oscar Arias of Costa Rica proposed a peace plan for Central America following the failure of the Contadora initiatives. Arias' plan became known as the Esquipulus II accords.

III. THE RIO TREATY: AN ANALYSIS OF THE INDEPENDENT VARIABLES

The previous chapter provided a summary of the extensive administrative and strategic thought that has been devoted to the idea of hemispheric defense. The culmination of this activity has been the Inter-American Treaty of Reciprocal Assistance (IATRA) or Rio Treaty. The Rio Treaty was the first joint security pact entered into by the United States after world War II. Invoked in 1947, it preceded the North Atlantic Treaty by two years. The Rio Treaty currently has twenty two signatories from both the Caribbean Region and Latin America.

This chapter will provide an analysis of the independent variables associated with the Rio Treaty using Holsti's eight criteria as set forth in Chapter I.

A. THE CASUS FOEDERIS

The IATRA declares that an armed attack against any American country would be considered an attack against all.[28] This catalyst for action has occurred on numerous occasions resulting from inter-hemispheric conflicts, but has never occurred as a result of intra-hemispheric conflict. Instances of the casus foederis coming into play are listed in Figure 5 below:

---

[28] Harold Molineu, *U.S. Policy Toward Latin America*, (Westview Press: Boulder) 1986, pp. 25, 26.

B. THE COMMITMENT OF SIGNATORIES

The nature of assistance which is to be rendered by the signatories in the event of armed attack is neither stated, nor automatic. Instead, the treaty calls for a meeting of national foreign ministers to determine the appropriate response which must be agreed upon by two-thirds vote.[29] A military response is left to the discretion of each signatory.

C. FORCE INTEGRATION

There have been some efforts made at force integration between United States and Latin American militaries. The primary military training in support of the Rio Treaty consists of "UNITAS",[30] an annual joint naval exercise which covers the area of the South Atlantic and South Pacific adjacent to Latin America. Several Latin American navies join the United States Navy in the yearly exercise which is a simulated South Atlantic and South Pacific war focusing on antisubmarine warfare. Much attention has been lavished on the social and political aspects of UNITAS, however its tactical and strategic significance has been the subject of debate.[31] In addition to UNITAS, the joint amphibious exercises VERITAS and CARBEX are

---

[29]Atkins, *Latin America in the International Political System*, p. 26.

[30]The origin of the term UNITAS is shrouded in controversy. Some say it is a Latin word meaning unity. Others say it is an acronym for "United Interamerican Antisumarine Warfare [Excercise]."

[31]Robert L. Scheina, *Latin America, a Naval History 1810-1987*, (Annapolis: Naval Institute Press, 1987) p. 175.

held at regular intervals by U.S., Argentine and Brazilian marines in the Caribbean.[32]

In addition to these training exercises, the United States government has made older U.S. Naval ships available to several Latin American countries by way of "no cost leasing". This is an arrangement whereby the receiving country finances costs for restoration of the ship to U.S. Navy standards, crew training, and obtaining spare parts. At the end of its useable life, the ship is either sold outright to the country for an extremely discounted price, or the country may sell the ship for scrap and give the proceeds to the U.S. government. Used aircraft have also been sold to several Latin American countries under the U.S. government's Foreign Military Sales program.

The United States has an intelligence exchange arrangement in place with selected Latin American countries, as well as a program enabling maritime operations independent of government involvement between U.S. and Latin American navies under the aegis of the "Common Strategic Consideration Papers". There are also navy-to-navy operations between Latin American countries independent of the United States navy. One example of this is "Fraterno," a yearly Argentine/Brazilian exercise[33] (See Appendix C for a list of joint U.S./Brazilian naval initiatives).

---

[32]Rene Luria, "The Brazilian Armed Forces, Budgets and Ambition Diverge," *International Defense Review*, July 1989, p. 933.
[33]Briefing by Captain Patrick Roth and CDR John G. Karas USN, Western Hemisphere Branch, Politico-Military Policy and Current Plans Division of OP-06, at U.S. Naval Postgraduate School, Monterey, Ca., 9 September 1990.

D. GEOGRAPHICAL SCOPE

The Northern and Southern boundaries of the Rio Treaty as spelled out at the Rio de Janeiro Conference in 1947 are from pole to pole. Canada and Greenland are included even though they are not signatories. The oceanic area included under the Rio Treaty is limited to the western portion of the South Atlantic. Any hostile action occurring in the eastern South Atlantic (which is the area that contains most of the trade routes to the United States) would not be covered under this treaty.[34]

E. DIVERGING OBJECTIVES

From its outset, the IATRA experienced multiple cases of diverging objectives. The treaty was essentially designed as a collective security agreement against Soviet threats to United States national security interests which was drafted with little regard to the Latin American interests or point of view.[35] The Latin American point of view was that no significant Soviet threat to the Western hemisphere existed, but if one materialized, the United States would counter it. Latin planners treated the agreement as a means of utilizing the United States to quell regional rivalries which were seen as a more imminent threat.[36] This factor spells a fundamental difference between the IATRA and the North Atlantic Treaty

---

[34]Kelly and Child, eds. *Geopolitics of the Southern Cone and Antarctica* , p. 218.
[35]Viron P. Vaky, et al., *Governance in the Western Hemisphere* (New York: Praeger, 1983), p. 165.
[36]James D. Barton, "The Viability of the Rio Treaty as a Basis for Coalition Defense", paper presented to the National War College, February, 1986, p. 6.

Organization (NATO) alliance. The Soviet threat has always been clearly perceived by all signatories of NATO, but has been remote to most Latin planners. Marxist-inspired revolution in Nicaragua, El Salvador and Grenada prompted only a lukewarm response from countries such as Brazil, Argentina, Chile and Mexico. These incidents, which were viewed by the United States as vital to security interests, were overshadowed in other Latin American countries by their own problems as well as reluctance by Latin American countries to side with the United States whose policy action is often characterized by vacillation and lack of positive action. As columnist Stephen Rosenfeld noted:

> While not wanting the hemisphere opened wider either to communist penetration or American intervention, the Latin fear is that their own fragile societies will be infected by the disease of violence and polarization which will distract from coping with need for modernization, an inherently destabilizing influence.[37]

This problem will be discussed further under "Threat Perception."

The United States has defined its interests in Latin America as being centered around debt reduction, anti-narcotics measures, support for democracy and environmental concerns.[38] These issues relate to domestic issues in the United States, and have a bearing on what the United States public will tolerate concerning alliances,

---

[37]Stephen S. Rosenfeld, "By Latins for Latins", *The Washington Post*, 17 January 86, p. A13.
[38]Secretary of State James A. Baker, *Latin America and the U.S.: A New Partnership*, Current Policy Bulletin No. 1160, United States Department of State, Bureau of Public Affairs, Washington D.C., 30 March 1989, p. 1.

military, and humanitarian aid. The Reagan administration's lack of support for Argentina during the Falklands conflict was seen by many Latin Americans as confirmation that the U.S. commitment to NATO was of higher interest than its commitment to the IATRA.[39]

By the beginning of 1988, the following sixteen Latin American countries had become full members of the Nonaligned Movement: Argentina, Belize, Bolivia, Chile, Colombia, Cuba, Ecuador, Grenada, Guyana, Jamaica, Nicaragua, Panama, Peru, St. Lucia, Suriname, and Trinidad-Tobago. The following eight countries attended as observers: Barbados, Brazil, Costa Rica, Dominica, El Salvador, Mexico, Uruguay, and Venezuela.[40] It should be noted that these countries support the Nonaligned Movement to varying degrees. For example, Cuba has been a leader in the Nonaligned Movement, whereas Argentina and Chile give the Movement less support.

F. THREAT PERCEPTION AND COLLATERAL THREATS

As mentioned earlier, the countries of Latin America have not shared the United States' concern over Soviet expansionism. The concept of security for many Latin American countries centers around domestic political unity, social progress and economic development. This feeling was demonstrated in the 1983 report of the Inter-American Dialogue:

---

[39] James D. Barton, "The Viability of the Rio Treaty as a Basis for Coalition Defense", paper presented to the National War College, February, 1986, p. 13.
[40] Atkins, *Latin America in the International Political System*, p. 81.

31

When Latin Americans think of security, most of them think of the internal challenges of national unity and development of border issues with neighboring states, and, in some cases, of the possibility of intervention by the United States. In the United States, the focus on security is external, global, and strategic. The United States generally seeks to assure political stability abroad, sometimes by supporting the status quo under sharp internal or regional challenge. Many Latin Americans feel that profound change is inevitable in their region, and that an emphasis on immediate stability is therefore misguided.[41]

Even in the United States, there is now a debate going on about the nature of the current threat. Both the "low threat view" and the "high threat/future threat" view will be presented below.

The most significant changes to United States national security from 1945 to 1980 occurred almost exclusively as a series of reactions to perceived Soviet threat. Perception of threat is a far more effective rallying cry to national security policy than support for democracy, human rights, or other such causes. Historically, when the United States has not perceived a threat, it has not taken security measures.

1. The Low Threat Argument

The United States Navy has, since World War II, been dedicated to countering the "Soviet Threat". If the "Declaration of Peace" made by Soviet leader Mikhail Gorbachev in 1988 is genuine, the national needs for naval preparedness are much different now than they have been in the past. By getting out of the cold war, the

---

[41]"The Americas at a Crossroads," report of the Inter-American Dialogue, Woodrow Wilson International Center for Scholars, April, 1983, pp. 40-41.

Soviets have admitted to the United States, the world, and themselves that they are a second-place superpower. Resources once dedicated to the "communist crusade" should now be dedicated inward. Even if Gorbachev fails, the majority of the Soviet Union's governmental attention must be focused inward in order to recover.

As observed by Captain Gerald G. O'Rourke, U.S. Navy (Retired):

> For the developing world, Soviet communism is hardly the political system to emulate...Lenin's doctrine is teetering on the edge of ideological and economic bankruptcy, most notably in Eastern Europe. The Soviet Union is now just another of the world's struggling nations, troubled by internal unrest, burdened by a massive military infrastructure, and bedeviled by the legacy of grandiose expansionist tendencies of the past. The Soviets have more than enough to keep them busy at home, not abroad, for a long time to come.[42]

The primary threat is no longer the Soviet Union, but third world countries practicing local adventurism, and inspired not by East-West ideological differences, but by religion or ethnicity. This being the case, there is no reason to maintain many of the current long-standing treaties and less reason to create any new ones. Unsophisticated third world militaries can be effectively countered by the less sophisticated forces of our military allies (and economic competitors) instead of involving the high-tech U.S. Navy.[43]

---

[42]Gerald G. O'Rourke, U.S. Navy (Retired), "Our Peaceful Navy", *U.S. Naval Institute Proceedings*, April 1989, p. 80.
[43]O'Rourke, "Our Peaceful Navy", p. 81.

The Defense Department has recently developed a new strategy that shifts security interests away from a major conflict with the Soviet Union in Europe, and toward potential regional conflicts such as the Iraqi conflict of August 1990. The blueprint was developed by Chairman of the Joint Chiefs of Staff, General Colin Powell and has been approved by Secretary of defense Richard Cheney and President George Bush. The new strategic thinking is that the Soviets will not be able to launch a major offensive in Western Europe for as long as two years once they withdraw from Eastern Europe. The new plan is consistent with the Bush administration's plan to reduce the military personnel strength by 25% and reduce spending by 10% over the next five years.[44]

The new strategy (which is currently being referred to as the "Reconstitution Strategy") is based on removing the bulk of U.S. forces from Europe and instead relying on forces based in the United States (both active and reserve) to deploy on short notice in case of major war with the Soviet Union.[45]

a. Implications of a Low Threat Environment on the Strategic Value of the South Atlantic

The importance of the South Atlantic to United States interests is a subject of controversy. The historic lack of any clear-cut defense planning or military alliances with countries sharing

---

[44]John D. Morrocco, "New Pentagon Strategy Shifts Focus From Europe to Regional Conflicts", *Aviation Week and Space Technology*, 13 August 90, p. 25.
[45]James J. Tritten, "America Promises to Come Back: A New National Strategy", NPS-NS-91-003, Naval Postgraduate School, Monterey, Ca., 26 December 1990, pp. 1-13.

interest in the freedom of the South Atlantic would seem to bear out the theory that the United States considers the area of secondary interest and does not perceive a threat to this region.

Much has been written regarding the strategic importance of the South Atlantic. Most Latin American writers place a far higher strategic value on the area than do writers of the United States. Indeed, a portion of the rationale given for Argentina taking back the Falklands rested on the belief that the South Atlantic held great strategic importance.

From a historical perspective, the South Atlantic was the scene of German U-boat activity in both World Wars. During the second World War, the northeast bulge of Brazil was referred to by the Brazilian military as "Brazil's stationary aircraft carrier", and was viewed as a "springboard to victory" with respect to controlling the area. Interest in the South Atlantic was rekindled with events of the mid 1970's which included the oil crisis of 1973, the increasing importance of Southeastern Atlantic oil sea lanes, the Cuban role in Angola, and the availability of west African ports to the Soviets.[46]

The following argument summarizes the thoughts of most writers who placed a high strategic value on control of the South Atlantic in the 1970's:

The rise of the supertanker, too large for the Suez Canal (and the closure of the canal after the 1967 Israel-Egypt war), had

---

[46]Jack Child, *Geopolitics and Conflict in South America*, (New York: Praeger, 1985), p. 125.

made the Cape of Good Hope route, and hence the South Atlantic, a key economic lifeline for Western Europe and the United States, which the expansion of the Soviet blue-water fleet put under constant threat. Adding to this the coming of the Alaskan supertankers, too large for the Panama Canal, and the possible threat to the Canal from left-wing control with the Panama Canal Treaty in 1977, Argentine writers saw the Southern Atlantic as a key global strategic zone, and were constantly puzzled by the low priority given the the region by the United States and western powers.[47]

Despite these events, the actual Soviet presence and interest in the South Atlantic remained low. Many analysts concluded that if the Soviets wanted to cut off South Atlantic oil supply lines to the west, they could more easily do so at the Persian Gulf or Strait of Hormuz. Nevertheless, the idea of a South Atlantic Treaty Organization (SATO) was postulated in 1976 shortly after the Cuban intervention of Angola. The concept of SATO stemmed from the fact that the NATO southern boundary stopped at the Tropic of Cancer and that the South Atlantic area was not covered by any other western treaty.[48]

SATO was originally envisioned to be a defense coalition between Argentina, Uruguay Brazil, and South Africa. Brazil rejected the idea primarily for two reasons: an inability to maintain a sizeable battle fleet in the South Atlantic, and a refusal to recognize

---

[47]Kelly and Child, eds. *Geopolitics of the Southern Cone and Antarctica* , pp. 227, 228.
[48]Child, *Geopolitics and Conflict* , p. 125.

Pretoria's apartheid government.   To do otherwise would have threatened Brazil's economic ties with black Africa.[49]

The strategic and economic importance of the South Atlantic has varied with historical events such as the closing of the Suez Canal and development of the super tanker as demonstrated by Figure 6 below:

---

[49]Luria, "The Brazilian Armed Forces, Budgets and Ambition Diverge," p. 933.

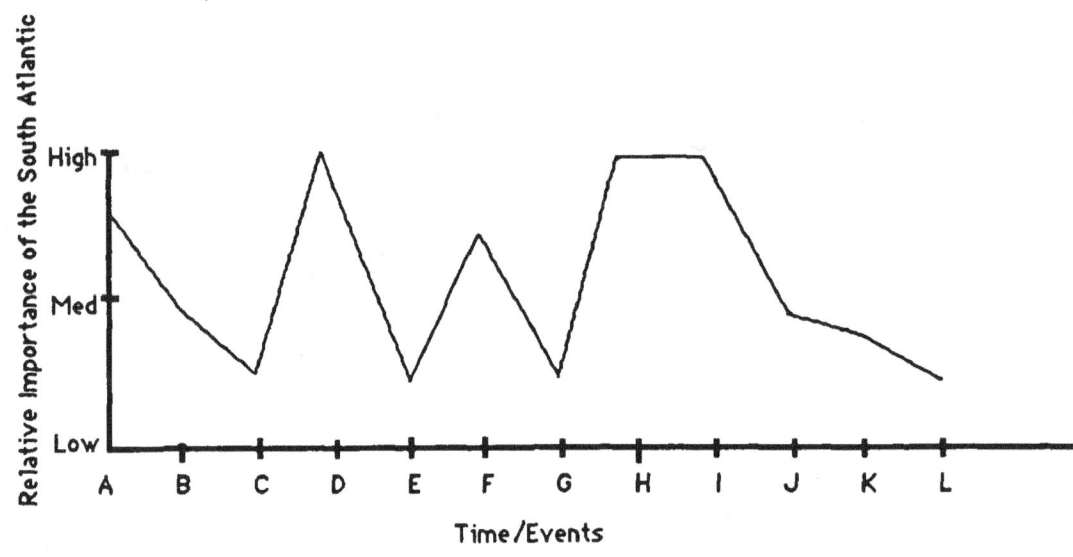

Key to Time/Events

A. **Pre 1869**--Neither Suez or Panama Canals built yet. South Atlantic only routes available.

B. **1869**--Suez Canal opens. Provides alternate trade route to going around Cape of Good Hope.

C. **1910**--Panama Canal Opens--Provides alternate route to Strait of Magellan, Beagle Channel, Drake Straits.

D. **1941**--World War II--Suez Canal closed for 76 days. Navigation hazardous through Suez while it was open. Allied shipping attacked in South Atlantic and Caribbean.

E. **1945**--World War II over.

F. **1956**--Suez War (Arab/Israeli). Suez Canal closed for five months.

G. **1957**--Suez War over. Canal opened.

H. **1967**--Arab/Israeli War. Suez Canal closed eight years due to mining. Also clogged with sunken ships, and remnants of tanks, airplanes and other equipment.

I. **1975**--Suez Canal opens.

J. **1976**--Dredging allows Supertankers one way use of Suez Canal (unloaded [shallower draft]).

K. **1980's**--Soviet and Cuban interest in Africa followed by decline of interest in late 1980s.

L. **1990**--Cold War over. Soviet and Cuban interest in Africa gone.

Figure 6:   The Changing Importance of the South Atlantic

38

For the last fifteen years, the South Atlantic has had a declining significance to the economic and strategic interests of the United States. Even at the height of Soviet expansionism in the 1970's and 1980's, the threat to these interests was low. The South Atlantic has not been, nor is it now, a primary theater of super power rivalry.[50]

2. The High Threat/Future Threat Argument

To many, recent events in the Soviet Union and Eastern Europe have seemingly ended the cold war. Others see the attitude that "the Soviet Union is gone as an adversary" as being extremely dangerous to United States national security posture.

The international environment has been transformed, but in what ways and to what extent is still a matter of speculation at best. Much depends on the success or failure of Mikhail Gorbachev and the three possible outcomes of his perestroika; succeeding, failing (with neither of these options being necessarily favorable to the United States), or continuing to "muddle through." If successful, the Soviet Union could emerge with a stronger, more efficient economy and a military more threatening than it has ever been. Failure of perestroika could lead to the reinstallation of totalitarian controls necessary to combat the resulting anarchy. Muddling through for five or ten years will give the United States more time to assess the

---

[50]Donald E. Nuechterlein, *America Overcommitted* (Lexington: The University Press of Kentucky, 1985), p. 159.

newly emerging world system and plan accordingly. The sincerity of Soviet "new thinking" can better be evaluated.[51]

Sea power will always remain crucial to the national security of the United States whether for countering third-world aggression, or strategically deterring the Soviet Union. Political Scientist Colin Gray noted that:

> Without freedom to use sea lines of communication (SLOCs) more or less at will, the United States would find itself shorn of much ability to take the initiative beyond North America (since such initiatives would entail passage over uncontrolled seas) and, given the growing interdependencies of economies, would find defense mobilization all but impossible to effect.[52]

Defense Secretary Dick Cheney said earlier this year:

> America's global military posture and leadership promotes an international environment in which free peoples and those seeking freedom can prosper . . . not only does our presence deter Soviet influence, it also can dampen regional arms competition and discourage local powers from seeking to dominate their neighbors.[53]

The fall of communism is not necessarily a cause for disarmament and demobilization. On the contrary, the fall of communism may be destabilizing. Peace in Europe will not be as secure as it was for the last forty years. A reunified Germany

---

[51]John L. Daily, "If Mikhail Muddles Through", *U.S. Naval Institute Proceedings*, June 1990, pp. 73, 74.
[52]Colin Gray, "Tomorrow's Forecast: Warmer/Still Cloudy", *U.S. Naval Institute Proceedings*, May 1990, pp. 40, 42.
[53]Gray, "Tomorrow's Forecast: Warmer/Still Cloudy", p. 42.

interacting in the economics and politics of a weakened Eastern Europe could be the kind of environment that has in the past led to war.[54]

As former Secretary of Defense Caspar Weinberger said,

> You will never know that you haven't got enough until it's too late to do anything about it. So yes, you err on the side of caution. You err on the side of having perhaps more than some people sitting down in some academic atmosphere will say you really require. I never felt sufficiently confident in my own ability, or anybody else's ability, to say what was precisely enough. So I always felt that we should have at least enough so that the Soviets, by any kind of calculation, would never feel that they could make a successful attack.

Weinberger has also warned of the possible Soviet tactic of using rhetoric to disengage the United States from Europe, a goal they have been striving for since he end of World War II. Unable to do it by threats, they are achieving their objective by using the argument that there is no longer a threat. Substantial military disengagement has not yet occurred.[55] Nothing has been done to change the nuclear equation. Soviet strategic forces, the only ones in the world that can destroy the United States, are being modernized and enhanced. Gorbachev has publicly stated that his aim is to make the Soviet military smaller, better, and more efficient.[56]

---

[54]Gray, "Tomorrow's Forecast: Warmer/Still Cloudy", p. 44.
[55]Gray, "Tomorrow's Forecast: Warmer/Still Cloudy", p. 51.
[56]General Colin Powell, "Crystal Balls Don't Always Help", *U.S. Naval Institute Proceedings*, May 90, p. 63.

In summary, the threats to the United States are both numerous and diverse. The Soviet Union is still a military superpower with highly capable conventional and nuclear capabilities. The world has never been free of hostility. The ongoing war in El Salvador, the restoration of democracy in Panama, coup attempts in the Philippines and Liberia and the Iraqi invasion of Kuwait are recent examples of this fact. The United States has commitments to its allies in Southeast Asia, Japan and Europe which need a military dimension to remain credible. The added burden on the military of fighting in the drug war takes away even more resources from other national security threats, and finally the worldwide commercial and security interests of the United States require a strong capable navy. Any assistance the United States can get from capable allies would not only be appreciated, but also greatly needed.

As Colin Powell said;

...the true 'peace dividend' is peace itself--the very first requirement of a democratic government. Peace comes about through maintenance of strength. So when people ask me what my strategy is, I say it's very simple. Peace through strength is my strategy. Peace is the objective and strength is the means.[57]

For these reasons, the United States military must remain strong. Coalition defense has always been the backbone of U.S. defense strategy. As President George Bush said, "we have never been able to 'go it alone' even in the early days of the cold war when

---

[57]Powell, "Crystal Balls Don't Always Help", p. 64.

our major allies were still suffering from the devastation and exhaustion of World War II." He went on to say, "we are prepared to share more fully with our allies and friends the responsibilities of global leadership".[58]

   a. *Implications of a High Threat/Future Threat Environment on the Strategic Value of the South Atlantic*

   There are five strategic "choke points" in the South Atlantic as indicated on Figure 7 below:

---

[58]President George Bush, *National Security Strategy of the United States*, The White House, March 1990, p. 15.

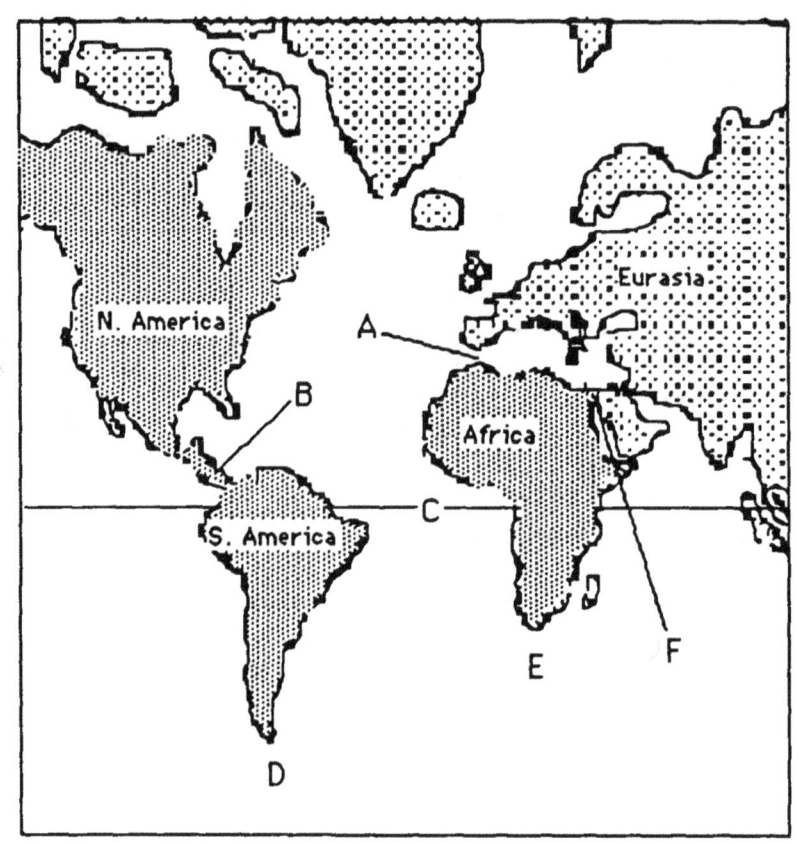

Key to Strategic Choke Points

A--Strait of Gibraltar   ▸-Drake Passage
B--Panama Canal   E--Cape of Good Hope
C--Atlantic Narrows   F--Suez Canal

Figure 7:   Strategic   Choke   Points

Maintaining freedom of navigation through these chokepoints is of vital interest, not only to the countries of Latin America, but also to the United States and its allies.

The most important maritime interest for the United States in the South Atlantic is the movement northward of Persian Gulf oil.[59] Approximately 66% of the oil shipped to Western Europe and about 26% of that shipped to the east coast of the United States goes through the South Atlantic.[60] Bauxite, beryllium, chromite, vanadium, cobalt, columbium, manganese, platinum, and tantalum also travel through the South Atlantic enroute to the United States and Britain.[61]

To further illustrate the area's importance to trade, 27,000 ships steam around the Cape of Good Hope per year transporting 90 percent of the west's petroleum, 70 percent of its minerals and 25 percent of its food imports.[62]

Figures 8 and 9 (below) show principal trade routes through the South Atlantic:

---

[59]Orlando Bonturi, *Brazil and the Vital South Atlantic*, (Washington D.C.: National Defense University Press, 1988), pp. 10, 11.
[60]Captain Joaquin Stella, "Stabilizing the Uneasy Atlantic", *U.S. Naval Institute Proceedings*, March 89, p. 59.
[61]Bonturi, *Brazil and the Vital South Atlantic*, pp. 10, 11.
[62]Bonturi, *Brazil and the Vital South Atlantic*, p. 18.

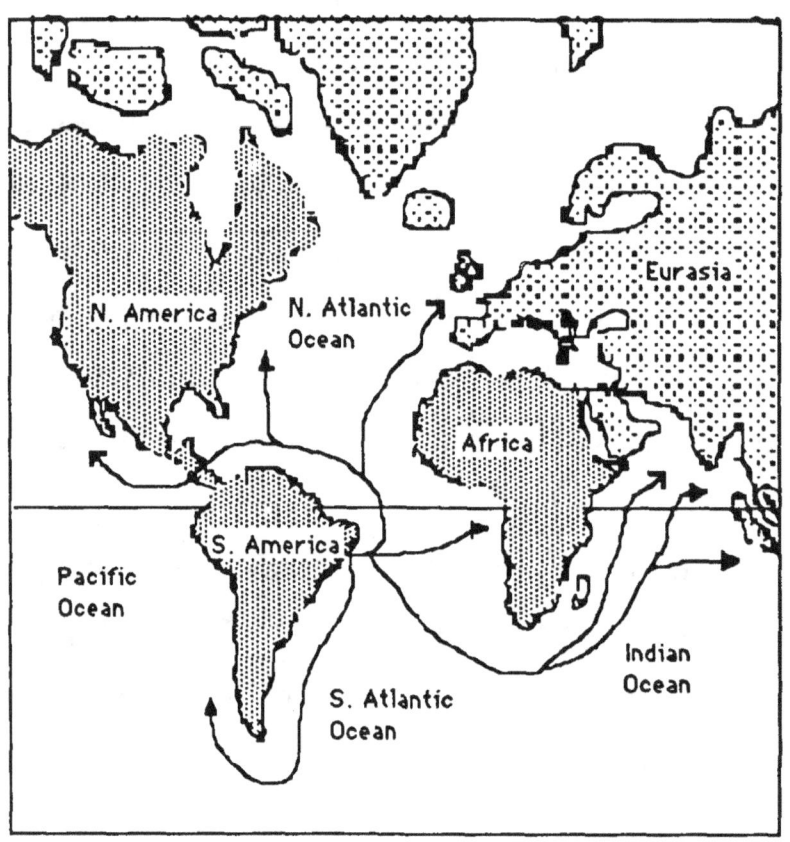

Source: Robert J. Branco, *The United States and Brazil*, (Washington D.C.: National Defense University Press, 1984), p. 78.

Figure 8:   South Atlantic Trade Routes of Brazilian Interest

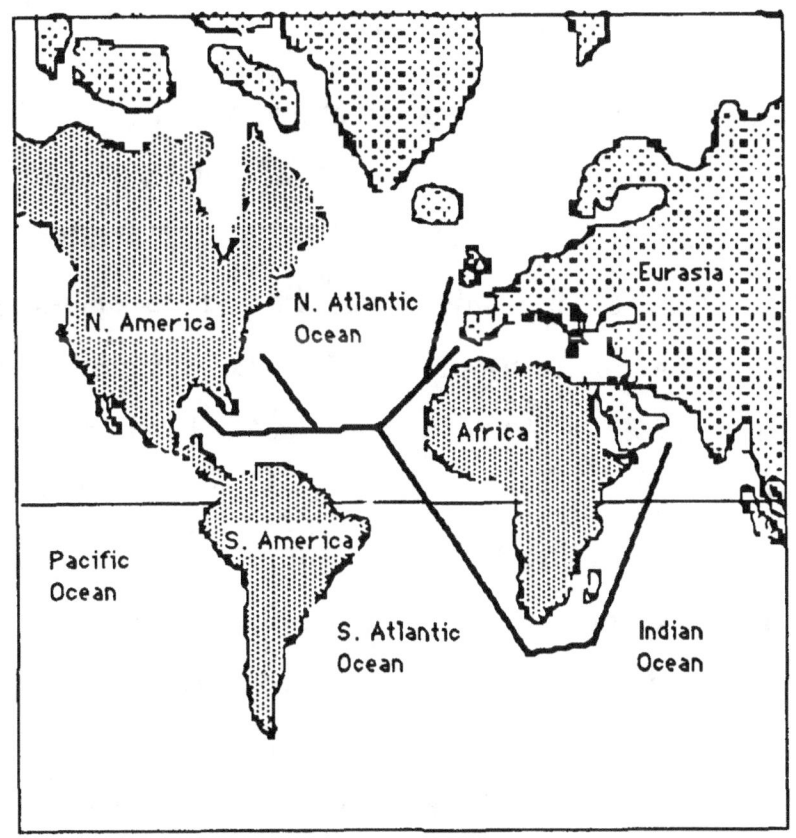

Source: Robert J. Branco, *The United States and Brazil*, (Washington D.C.: National Defense University Press, 1984), p. 78.

Figure 9: South Atlantic Trade Routes of North American and European Interest

In terms of national security, the South Atlantic's strategic significance would increase with the closing of the Suez or Panama Canals, or in the event of military conflict in Europe or the Indian Ocean.

From a naval strategy point of view, former U.S. Chief of Naval Operations, Admiral James D. Watkins has expressed concern that Soviet SSBNs, instead of staying in geographically confined "bastions" close to the Soviet Union, may instead be operating or be planning to operate in Southern waters. His views were seconded by former Commander-in-Chief Atlantic Fleet (CINCLANTFLT) Admiral Harry D. Train II. Train has argued that the South Atlantic, being light on anti-submarine warfare patrols and capabilities would offer a relatively safe patrol area to which the Soviet Union could deploy its SSBNs. Train cites several years of Soviet hydrographical research and periodic deployment of Delta Class SSBNs as supporting evidence that the Soviets would station submarines in these waters.[63]

In summary, threat to the area of the South Atlantic is not well defined at this point. Elements of both the low threat and the high threat/future threat arguments appear to be valid. The United States government seems to be leaning in favor of the low threat argument with respect to the Soviet Union by virtue of Washington's consideration of the new "Reconstitution Strategy." However, regional threats are very real as demonstrated by the Middle East

---

[63]Jan S. Breemer, "The Soviet Navy's SSBN Bastions: New Questions Raised", *RUSI Journal of the Royal United Services Institute for Defence Studies*, June 1987, pp. 39-43.

war of January and February, 1991. Internal regional threats such as narco-trafficking, narco-terrorism and insurgency directly affect most countries in the area of the South Atlantic. Extra hemispheric regional problems such as the Iraqi invasion of Kuwait also affect the economies of these countries.

Whether or not a military partnership between the United States and Brazil should be based on some aspect of the "Reconstitution Strategy" or on aspects of regional threat, will be investigated in Chapter V.

G. COMPATIBILITY OF SOCIAL AND POLITICAL VALUES

All Latin American members of the alliance are now generally capitalistic, democratic, Christian countries which in a broad sense make them socially and politically compatible with the United States. There have been numerous instances of military dictatorships coming to power in countries throughout Latin America, but as Robert Wesson has put it, the pendulum seems to be swinging more and more in favor of democratically elected governments.[64]

H. NUCLEAR WEAPON CAPABILITIES OF SIGNATORIES

No Latin American country currently has nuclear weapon capability. Some analysts believe Brazil and Argentina will have this capability by the year 2000, but both countries have denied the

---

[64]Robert Wesson, ed., *The Latin American Military Institution*, (New York: Praeger, 1986), p. xiii.

desire to use nuclear technology for anything but peaceful purposes (See further discussion in Chapter V).

IV. THE RIO TREATY: AN EVALUATION OF THE DEPENDENT VARIABLE

The following chapter summarizes the information presented in the previous chapter, and is arranged according to Holsti's eight criteria:

A. IS THE CASUS FOEDERIS (CATALYST FOR ACTION) SPECIFIED?

Yes. Military measures can only be taken in response to armed attack on one of the signatories.

B. IS THE TYPE OF ACTION TO BE TAKEN BY SIGNATORIES SPECIFIED?

No. It is neither stated nor automatic. Use of military force is optional to each signatory.

C. ARE PLANS IN PLACE TO USE INTEGRATED FORCES?

No. Some integration has taken place in the form of Foreign Military Sales to Latin American countries and occasional coordinated operations between signatories. However, the overall ability of these forces to integrate effectively is questionable due to sporadic participation in training operations, a small number of training operations, and a generally low military capability of most signatories.

D. IS THERE A SPECIFIC GEOGRAPHICAL SCOPE?

Yes. The geographical scope is from pole to pole, including all of the continental American states, Alaska, and adjacent islands with the exception of Hawaii. It covers Canada and Greenland even though they are not signatories.

E. ARE ALLIANCE MEMBERS FREE OF DIVERGING OBJECTIVES?

No. The cause of most divergences centers around the Latin quest for economic security which has pre-empted an interest in military security.

F. IS THERE A CLEAR PERCEPTION OF THREAT WITH NO COLLATERAL THREAT TO ONE OR A FEW ALLIES?

No. At the treaty's formation, the United States was more interested in unified defense against Soviet threat. The United States is now unsure of the current threat status. The Latin Americans have been more interested in regional stability and economic progress.

G. IS THERE COMPATIBILITY OF SOCIAL AND POLITICAL VALUES BETWEEN THE ALLIES?

Yes. All signatories generally are Christian, democratic, and capitalistic with few exceptions.

H. DO MEMBERS OTHER THAN THE UNITED STATES HAVE NUCLEAR WEAPONS?

No. The United States, through non-proliferation measures has attempted to thwart Argentine and Brazilian development of nuclear weapons (See Chapter V).

The preceding eight criteria are presented as independent variables in the hypothesis testing matrix for the case of the Rio Treaty on Figure 10 below:

INDEPENDENT VARIABLES ⇨

A	B	C	D	E	F	G	H
Casus Foederis precise?	Commitment precise and auto-matic?	Force integra-tion?	Geo-graphical scope precise?	Free of Diverg-ing Objec-tives?	Clear threat percep-tion. No collat-eral threats?	Compat-ibility of social and political values?	Members have Nuc Weaps?
YES	NO	NO	YES	NO	NO	YES	NO

DEPENDENT VARIABLE ⇨

= Non-Viable Alliance

Figure 10:

Hypothesis Testing Matrix: Rio Treaty

54

As demonstrated in the matrix, the Rio Treaty is not a viable alliance as explained by negative responses in categories B, C, E, and F.

Categories B, C, and E are problems which have been in place since the Treaty's inception. Although Latin America's position with regard to category F (threat perception) has been debatable for some time, the events of 1989 in the Soviet Union and Eastern Bloc have now made even the United States' position questionable.

V. EVALUATING THE OPTIONS FOR U.S. POLICY

In its present condition, the IATRA is not a viable basis for coalition defense. Those adherents of the "low threat" argument would argue that this is not a problem since there is no need for the alliance anyway. On the other hand, proponents of the "high threat/future threat" argument would say that something should be done about the treaty, even if the present situation does not seem to support a change in the status quo.

There are three options with regard to the Rio Treaty. One has already been mentioned; write the IATRA off as a worthless treaty for a nonexistent threat, and do nothing. The other two options are to revitalize the existing treaty, or to replace the treaty with carefully selected bilateral defense agreements.

A. REVITALIZING THE EXISTING TREATY

In order to revitalize the treaty, categories B, C, and E of the hypothesis testing matrix must be dealt with. Four possible means of correcting these categories are listed below: ·

•Redefine the casus foederis to include such issues as insurgencies, drug trafficking, narco-terrorism, and defense of overseas interests, in addition to military attack.

•Re-write the vaguely worded commitment to mandate specific military responses to specifically worded catalysts.

•Increase the level of force integration by increasing the number of training exercises between signatories, increasing inter-

56

operability of weapons systems, and installing a command structure patterned after NATO.

The most important category is category F, "threat perception." By expanding the casus foederis to include counterinsurgency, narco-terrorism, and defense of overseas interests, the threat perception may become broader to some of the countries. For other countries, it may not. Countries that show no interest in the new initiative to revitalize the treaty should be allowed to leave it.

A possible danger to this approach is that no countries may show interest (or none of the countries with the most substantial militaries) in the new initiative, thus causing the treaty to collapse altogether. This would not be desirable. Although the treaty is non-viable as a defense mechanism, it still provides a web of personal contacts which could be useful at a future date.

Even if the smaller countries agreed to this proposal, their usefulness for a joint naval partnership is marginal. Argentina, Brazil and possibly Chile are the only Latin American navies that have the capability to project force outside of their territorial waters. Assigning the role of defending overseas interests to any Latin American navies other than these would require major augmentation of their capabilities, a measure unlikely to be undertaken either by the individual countries or the United States, given the magnitude of upgrade required.

A better course of action would be to keep the Rio Treaty in place, but add focused partnerships with the three most capable navies.

B. KEEP THE TREATY, BUT ADD BILATERAL AGREEMENTS

This option entails decreasing emphasis on the treaty and instead pursuing a program of bilateral military alliances. These new bilateral alliances would be faced with the same problems that the Rio Treaty is faced with, therefore the new agreements would similarly need to address categories B, C, and E of the hypothesis testing matrix as noted in the previous example. The bilateral agreement technique has the following advantages:

•It is constructive, i.e. does not force a country's hand to make a drastic change in its defense orientation as the previous option does. The country either accepts or rejects the new proposal without the fear of being "kicked out" of the existing alliance.

•It is easier to manage in a diverse region. Countries would be hand picked. Those that have weak or inefficient military establishments would be overlooked.

•It allows the United States to concentrate assets rather than spread itself too thin by trying to "prop up" many diverse militaries.

•It avoids the possibility of total collapse inherent in the previous option.

•It could be used to link Latin participation with some sort of incentive program such as more favorable agreements on foreign military sales from the United States.

The Rio treaty should not be totally ignored if this option is implemented. Rather it can remain in place, not viable militarily, but nonetheless, providing a web of contacts which allow open dialogue with Latin American navies.

The obvious first choice of a bilateral partner for this option is Brazil for the reasons given in Chapter I. A partnership with Brazil could be established on a trial basis, and if successful, another country, possibly Argentina could be added at a future date. This proposal would not be without its problems, and a few of the more obvious are presented below.

1. Brazil's Capabilities

Even though Brazil possesses the largest and most capable navy of all the signatories, its sea power projection and antisubmarine warfare (ASW) capabilities are *currently* inadequate to assume a credible position of integrated alliance with the United States Navy (see Appendix B for an overview of Brazilian naval assets). The antiquated electronics in Brazil's antisubmarine warfare S-2 Tracker aircraft squadrons and lack of carrier-based strike and fighter aircraft capability limit its utility as a maritime defense partner with the United States.[65]

Nevertheless, if one were to choose from a list of third world navies with regional force projection capability, Brazil, Argentina and India would be the only choices available (see Appendix A). The

---

[65] Brazil's only aircraft carrier, the "Minas Gerais" is currently antisubmarine warfare capable only, and has no compatible strike or fighter aircraft in its airwing.

59

Brazilian navy is actively attempting to upgrade its capability. Plans for a nuclear submarine continue, and three IKL-209 (Type 1400) class West German submarines are to be built at the Arsenal de Marinha do Rio de Janeiro. In 1989 Brazil acquired four Garcia FF-1040 class frigates and one Thomaston (LSD-28) class dock landing ship from the United States. The Brazilian air force is currently in the process of re-engining twelve of its Grumman Tracker antisubmarine warfare planes with modern turboprop engines.[66]

Of concern to the Brazilian navy is the continually shrinking military budget which has fallen from 1.5% to .3% of the Gross National Product (GNP) over the last twenty years.[67] The proposed 1990 budget was .2% of GNP; the lowest in forty years. This makes the future of Brazil's naval modernization program uncertain.[68]

The United States would probably have to subsidize the required build-up of the Brazilian navy if a credible defense role is assigned to Brazil. This subsidy could be in the form of discount prices on the sale of equipment, or more favorable lend-lease arrangements using mothballed United States ships and aircraft which may become available in the event of a United States naval force reduction.

[66]Aviation Week and Space Technology, January 7, 1991.
[67]World Military Expenditures and Arms Transfers 1971-1980, United States Arms Control and Disarmament Agency, (Washington D.C.: U.S. Government Printing Office, 1983), p. 41;
World Military Expenditures and Arms Transfers 1989, United States Arms Control and Disarmament Agency, (Washington D.C.: U.S. Government Printing Office, 1990), p. 39.
[68]Robert L. Scheina, "Latin American Navies", U.S. Naval Institute Proceedings, March 90, p. 112.

2. Brazil's Past Stance on Alliances

Brazil has demonstrated an aversion to automatic alliances, but has indicated that if the need for an alliance ever arose, it would occur naturally. At the Center for Brazilian Strategic Studies, Rear Admiral Mario Cesar Flores (now Brazil's Minister of the Navy) discussed the Brazilian perspective on this issue:

> The association with the North Americans and the West in general, in whose strategic camp we will naturally be contained, a more sensible participation in the western portion of the South Atlantic, should occur naturally at the opportune occasion, not seeming to be compulsorily promoted in a formal way in a premature epoch.[69]

The negative response to President Ronald Reagan's suggestion of a military partnership in both the South Atlantic and Central America,[70] and Brazil's disinterest in establishing a joint-use military base on Trindade Island in the South Atlantic[71] is further evidence that it is not interested in a joint defense agreement with the United States.

Reasons for Brazilian disinterest may include a lack of perceived threat in the area, the distaste of being subordinated to the United States in a "junior partner" relationship, the belief that the United States will protect the South Atlantic regardless of any

---

[69]Robert J. Branco, *The United States and Brazil*, (Washington D.C.: National Defense University Press, 1984), p. 79.

[70]*Brazil: A Country Study*, p. 282.

[71]Wayne A. Selcher, "Brazil and the Southern Cone", in *South America Into the 1990s*, ed., G. Pope Atkins, (Boulder: Westview Press, 1990), p. 117.

partnerships, and a wariness of United States' commitment to treaties and alliances after the Falkland/Malvinas war.

Not only has Brazil rejected a U.S. proposal for a South Atlantic defense coalition, but it rejected a similar proposal from Argentina to join with Uruguay and South Africa in a coalition defense agreement in 1973. Brazil declined the offer for two reasons: an inability to maintain a sizeable battle fleet in the South Atlantic, and its non-recognition of Pretoria's apartheid government.[72]

The only treaty Brazil has been interested in regarding the South Atlantic is one that it cosponsored with Argentina and other Latin American and African nations to create a zone of peace and cooperation in the area. The proposal was adopted by the United Nations in 1986, and attempts to remove Latin America from superpower conflict as well as eliminate nuclear weapons in the region.[73]

Brazil's aversion to automatic alliances may be modified under the proper circumstances, such as linking debt reduction or discounted military sales to an active role in defense burdensharing. Brazilian naval officers have promoted defense of the South Atlantic in the past as a possible way to expand their mission[74] and modernize their navy. There has been cooperation between the

---

[72]Luria, "The Brazilian Armed Forces, Budgets and Ambition Diverge,", p. 933.
[73]Roberto Russell, "Argentina: Ten Years of Foreign Policy", in Kelly and Child, eds., p. 77.
[74]Child, *Geopolitics and Conflict* , p. 37.

navies of both the United States and Brazil despite Brazil's stance on alliances (See Appendix C for details of that cooperation). It is possible therefore, that the Brazilian navy would welcome the idea of a defense partnership with the United States, which could be used to put pressure on the Brazilian government to alter its aversion to automatic alliances.

A number of geopolitical factors make the desirability of a defense partnership with the United States questionable from the Brazilian standpoint. A large part of Brazil's rapprochement with Argentina was based on demonstrating independence from the United States. Brazil may be unwilling to jeopardize the advances it has made by rekindling a junior partner status with the United States.

3. Brazil's Geopolitical Considerations

Rivalry between Brazil and Argentina has its roots in colonial times and arose from trade, border and sphere of influence disputes. Although relations have been steadily improving over the last decade, an atmosphere of competition is likely to continue for some time. The main point of uneasiness rests primarily with Argentina's sense of frustration at not achieving what it considered to be its destiny of primacy in South America.

A large source of friction and competition between the two countries centers around their relations with the three so-called "buffer states" of Uruguay, Paraguay, and Bolivia. Together, these three countries form the La Plata Basin System because they all contain tributaries which empty into the La Plata river. The La Plata Basin is an area of geopolitical competition between Argentina and Brazil due to competing desires to monopolize the production of iron and energy reserves (coal, petroleum and hydroelectricity).[75]

Brazil has made important economic and political inroads to these countries in recent years, most significantly in Paraguay with mutual cooperation on hydroelectric projects.[76] More recent sources of Argentine/Brazilian conflict have been Brazil's burgeoning interest in portions of Antarctica to which Argentina has already laid claim, the technology race in developing nuclear power, and competition in regional markets for their respective arms industries.[77]

Finally, a less tangible but no less real source of conflict, is the stereotypical views each country holds of the other. The Argentine elites are said to have a self perception of racial and cultural superiority toward the racially mixed Brazil.[78] Brazil, on the other hand, from the worst stereotypical perspective, views Argentina as a country characterized by political instability, haughtiness, lack of discipline, military cruelty, economic stagnation, and organizational weakness.[79]

---

[75]Philip Kelly and Jack Child, eds., *Geopolitics of the Southern Cone and Antarctica*, (Boulder and London: Lynne Rienner Publishers, 1988) p. 146.

[76]Brazil: A Country Study, p. 280.

[77]Jack Child, *Geopolitics in the Southern Cone*, (New York: Praeger, 1985), pp. 98-104.

[78]Wayne A. Selcher, "Brazilian-Argentine Relations in the 1980s; From Wary Rivalry to Friendly Competition", *Journal of Interamerican Studies and World Affairs*, Summer 1985, p. 26.

[79]Selcher, "Brazilian-Argentine Relations", p. 27.

The "economic miracle" of Brazil during the late 1960's and early 1970's contrasted with the steady decline of Argentina and brought about a pragmatic shift of Argentine attitude concerning the years old rivalry with Brazil. The idea began to take shape in Buenos Aires that Argentina was a second rate power compared to Brazil and would remain so unless an atmosphere of cooperation between the countries prevailed.[80] As political scientist Philip Kelly noted:

> Brazilian-Argentine rivalry has hindered Southern Cone integration, created possibilities for serious, indigenous nuclear weapons development, jeopardized peaceful settlement of disputes in the region intensified competition among Southern Cone states for control of the Antarctic, and prevented Brazil from distancing itself from the United States. Above all, the cleavage between Brazil and Argentina has forestalled a more assertive role for the region in world strategic relationships, a checkmating effect that has kept the entire area fixed to the global political and economic periphery.[81]

Rapprochement between Brazil and Argentina began with the signing of the Tripartite Agreement on the Corpus-Itaipu hydroelectric projects between Argentina, Paraguay and Brazil in 1979. The change in Argentine governance from a military to civilian regime marked a return to a close relationship with neighboring Latin American countries which had been de-emphasized during the military junta of 1976 to 1983. The foreign

---

[80]Kelly and Child, eds., *Geopolitics of the Southern Cone and Antarctica* , p. 74.
[81]Kelly and Child, eds., *Geopolitics of the Southern Cone and Antarctica* , p. 116.

policy of the Alfonsin administration centered on the following pillars:

- The consolidation of peace and the discouragement of all types of arms races;
- Opposition to any doctrine which subordinated Latin America to the strategic objectives of the superpowers;
- Promotion of representative government on the continent;
- Promotion of policies which regionalized problems and their solutions;
- Integration within Latin America.[82]

Other examples of rapprochement between Brazil and Argentina included agreements in matters of nuclear, technical and industrial cooperation. A formal military-industrial agreement between the two countries has not been signed. However, an increasing number of bilateral agreements between Brazil and Argentina may eventually put an end to their historical rivalry. In November 1990, Brazil and Argentina signed a nuclear power treaty which led President Collor of Brazil to make the following comments regarding the significance of the agreement:

The declaration that we have just signed merits, like few others, being termed as historic. It marks the beginning of a new phase in our bilateral relations to the nuclear field, creates the possibility of joint negotiations with the International Atomic

---

[82]Kelly and Child, eds., *Geopolitics of the Southern Cone and Antarctica* , p. 85.

Energy Agency [IAEA], and is a step toward the signing of the Tlatelolco Treaty.[83]

Both countries are reportedly working together on the development of fast breeder reactors. Brazilian President Jose Sarney's visit to the Argentine uranium enrichment plant in July 1987 led to speculation that the two countries would eventually team up in their plans to develop nuclear submarines. Indeed, the astronomical expense and high risk of such a program seems to lend itself to an international partnership.[84]

Despite the current atmosphere of cooperation in the Southern Cone, both countries are aware that old rivalries could be rekindled in Antarctica or the South Atlantic. Both of these regions have been in dispute by several different countries for a number of years.[85] The discovery of oil or valuable minerals in these areas could easily stoke quietly smoldering rivalries into a flare up.

Brazil's culture, size, fascination with the United States, geopolitical rivalries and distances of major population centers from Spanish Latin America are factors which have separated it from neighboring countries. These factors are seen as having been detrimental to Brazil's ability to project influence, and its ability to become integrated within Latin America.

---

[83]"Collor Address on Treaty With Argentina," (in Portuguese), *Folha de Sao Paulo*, 29 Nov 90, p. A 6, translated and reported in FIBIS LAT-90-236, 7 December 1990, p. 28.

[84]Eduardo Italo Pesce, "Brazil's Silent Service", *U.S. Naval Institute Proceedings*, March 1989, p. 66.

[85]Among them, Brazil, Chile, Argentina, Great Britain, and many other countries, both developed and undeveloped worldwide.

In March of 1977, Brazil refused $60 million dollars of U.S. military aid which was linked to human rights issues. It also denounced the Interamerican Treaty of Mutual Assistance, and expelled the U.S. naval mission.[86] This was not merely a response to an isolated incident. It was also a signal to the rest of Latin America that Brazil wanted to end the perception of being a U.S. proxy so that integration with its neighbors would be facilitated. Brazil recognizes that its latitude in the western hemisphere can be ultimately restricted by pressure from Washington if United States security interests are threatened. It is therefore to Brazil's advantage to resist close political or military identification with the United States.

Both Argentine and Chilean geopolitical thinking have a strong maritime component with their interests in southern passages, the Malvinas, and Antarctica. A joint naval partnership between Brazil and the United States could be viewed as being threatening to Argentina's national interest. Argentina may fear the partnership would replace its current rivalry against Chile and Brazil with a new rivalry against Chile, Brazil and the United States. This would not be conducive to southern cone integration. Braz' has rejected the idea of a joint military partnership with the United States in the past, and may do so in the future as long as southern cone integration remains a keystone to its national interest.

---

[86]Robert L. Scheina, *Latin America, a Naval History 1810-1987*, (Annapolis: Naval Institute Press, 1987) pp. 171, 172.

On the other hand, if Argentina did see its national interest jeopardized with the formation of a Brazil, U.S. and defacto Chilean alliance, a possible solution to this would be to include Argentina in the partnership as well. After all, Argentina envisioned the idea of the South Atlantic Treaty Organization (see Chapter III), to which Brazil declined membership because of political considerations and constraints in naval resources. The navies of each country do not seem to have a problem with geopolitical rivalry as demonstrated by their willingness to cooperate on their yearly maritime exercise "Fraterno".

Argentina might also see a benefit of being linked to the United States in a maritime capacity to protect its interests with regard to Chile and its claims in Antarctica. This would no doubt upset the Chileans who regard their Brazilian connection as important for countering Argentina. The Brazil/Chile connection however is informal and therefore does not represent a vital interest to Brazil. Brazil may agree to include Argentina in the defense partnership for this reason.

4. Problematic U.S./Brazilian Bilateral Issues

There are several bilateral issues between the United States and Brazil that represent diverging objectives and may make a military alliance tenuous;

a. Debt and Trade

Brazil put a moratorium on its debt servicing in 1987, but announced plans to partially lift the moratorium in December

1990. For the first three months of 1991, Brazil plans to pay 30 percent of the interest from its $63 billion private bank debt. Total interest arrears to commercial banks now total $8.3 billion.[87]

If Brazil were unable to surmount its massive debt problems which have thus far shown no signs of real recovery, the economic impact would reverberate throughout the world system. Compounding these problems are heavy debt servicing, rising costs for many of Brazil's imports, northern protectionism against its exports and a falling demand for its products.[88]

In addition to debt problems creating friction between the United States and Brazil, trade imbalances have also contributed to economic problems between the two countries. In 1989 there was a $4.2 billion trade imbalance between the United States and Brazil in Brazil's favor.[89]

b. Security

Brazil's military industrial complex has sold weapons to regimes hostile to the United States such as Iraq, Libya and Iran. On a number of occasions, protests by the United States have resulted in modifications of this policy.

The primary issue of conflict is Brazil's insistence of acquiring ballistic missiles and related technology. The United States

---

[87]Christina Lamb, "Brazil will 'partially lift' Moratorium", *Financial Times of London*, December 19, 1990.

[88]Abraham Lowenthal, "Rethinking US Interests in the Western Hemisphere", *Journal of Interamerican Studies and World Affairs*, vol 29, Spring 1987, pp. 10, 11.

[89]"Direction of Trade Statistics Yearbook", International Monetary Fund, Publication Services, Washington, D.C., 1990, p. 403.

is concerned that Brazil may have nuclear warhead and delivery capability by the year 2000. Both Brazilian Foreign Minister Francisco Rezek and National Commission of Nuclear Energy president Jose Luiz de Carvalho Santana have denied that Brazil would use nuclear technology for military purposes. Both refused to comment on a recent report released by the Carnegie Foundation for International Peace in Washington D.C. that Brazil and Argentina smuggled technology from West Germany to expand their nuclear weapons capabilities.[90] Both Brazil and Argentina formally renounced the manufacture of nuclear weaponry just prior to president Bush's South American visit in November 1990. Both countries however have yet to announce intentions to abide by either the Nuclear Non-Proliferation Treaty or the Treaty of Tlatelolco, two regimes aimed at keeping Latin America free of atomic weapons.[91] The United States has restricted its technology to Brazil under the Missile Technology Control Regime (MTCR). Members of the MTCR include the United States, Canada, France, Germany, Italy, Japan, Britain, Sweden and Switzerland (the MTCR does not include the Soviet Union and China).

Brazil has gone to both France and Germany for missile technology under the guise of acquiring space systems technology. Although they are MTCR members, France and Germany do not

---

[90]Executive News Services, APn 04/17 2213, Brazil-Nuclear, The Associated Press, 1990.
[91]Shirly Christian, "Argentina and Brazil Renounce Atomic Weapons", *The New York Times*, 29 November 1990.

associate space programs with ballistic missile programs to the same extent that the United States does. France has given Brazil dated rocket launching technology.

Chinese missiles use different rocket propellants than those the Brazilians are planning to acquire, and the Soviet Union so far has not shown interest in sharing its missile technology with Brazil.[92]

c. Theft of Intellectual Property Rights

The United States has accused Brazil of making products and profits (mostly in the pharmaceutical and computer industries) from pirated United States technology and giving the United States nothing in return. As punishment, Washington placed Brazil on the Intellectual Property Rights Watch List and imposed 100% tariffs on Brazilian paper products, drugs and electronics items although such measures were contrary to the rules of the General Agreement on Tariffs and Trade (GATT). Within the GATT framework, service and intellectual property rights are not recognized as having legal ownership.

d. The Amazon Issue

Most industrialized countries, as well as the World Bank and International Development Bank are pressuring Brazil to cease its deforestation of the Amazon. So far, 5% of the jungle has been

---

[92]Scott D. Tollefson, "Brazil, the United States, and the Missile Technology Control Regime". NPS-56-90-006, paper prepared for the Naval Postgraduate School, Monterey, Ca., March 1990, p. 82.

deforested and in December of 1988, Chico Mendez, a leading crusader against Amazon development, was killed by developers.

President Jose Sarney's (1985-1990) initial response to anti-development pressure was antagonistic, proclaiming that "no one has the right to tell Brazil how to run its country." He later softened his rhetoric and instituted several measures which included suspending tax incentives and banning timber exports as preliminary measures to discourage development of the Amazon Basin.

Current president Fernando Collor de Mello has made environmental reform a major goal. He is enforcing a federal court order banning miners from the Amazon basin, instituted in October of 1989. Following a helicopter flight over the area, Collor ordered several crude landing strips blown up to prevent the illegal entry of miners on federally protected lands.[93] The rain forest continues to be cut down despite these moves. Further destruction of the rain forest could aggravate relations between the United States and Brazil to the point that congressional support for a bilateral defense partnership could be hampered.

e. General Agreements

Brazil has shown a distinct preference for going its separate way to achieve its own interests on such matters as trade relations and international agreements. Brazil's dependence on Middle Eastern petroleum which began in the 1970s, has driven a wedge between it and the United States on the Arab-Israeli conflict,

---

[93]"Blowup in the Rain Forest", *Time*, April 90, p. 59.

and has led Brazil to develop ties with various Arab countries, some hostile to the United States.[94]   Additionally, Brazil no longer automatically supports the United States on international issues.   In the 1985 session of the United Nations General Assembly, Brazil was among three Latin American countries that voted with the United States the least number of times (less than 16%).[95]

From the standpoint of many Latin Americans, the deforestation and arms sales issues should be of no concern to the "Yankees."   The deforestation issue is regarded as an example of the Yankees applying a dual set of standards to the problem.   The United States "raped" its own countryside, but now takes a condescending and paternalistic view of the Latin Americans when they do the same thing.

The remaining issues have come about as a result of U.S. involvement in Latin affairs.   To the problem of debt, a common Latin American explanation heard is that the United States caused the debt by offering loans with unrealistically low interest rates.   The drug supply problem is seen not as a Latin American problem of supply, but as a North American problem of demand.   To the arms transfer problem, many Latin Americans would argue that Washington has also sold weapons to countries which have later become hostile to the United States.

---

[94]Lowenthal, "Rethinking US Interests in the Western Hemisphere", p. 6.
[95]Lowenthal, "Rethinking US Interests in the Western Hemisphere", p. 7.

Although these issues are of concern inasmuch as they affect relations between the governments of both countries, they seem to be getting less important. Initiatives have been taken on both sides to try to reduce the problems, such as President Bush's Enterprise for the Americas Initiative, which is aimed at forming a western hemispheric free trade zone that may in turn help to alleviate Brazilian debt. Recent statements by President Collor indicate Brazilian support for non-proliferation of nuclear weapons. In addition, there has been some progress made on the deforestation issue.

These issues have had some effect on navy to navy relations as demonstrated by the lack of Maritime Interest Papers between Brazil and the United States. Maritime Interest Papers (also called Common Strategic Consideration papers) are currently in place between the United States and Argentina, Chile, Colombia, Ecuador, Peru, Uruguay and Venezuela. These papers allow navy to navy operations to take place without government involvement. The U.S. State Department disapproved the signing of Maritime Interest Papers due to problems with Brazilian trade practices in the 1980s. These trade problems have been partially rectified. However, there are still no Maritime Interest Papers in place between Brazil and the United States.[96] Notwithstanding, the Brazilian military seems to have less of an aversion to bilateral accords than the government does, as evidenced

---

[96]These papers have not been signed as of February 1991.

by an increasing number of naval bilateral initiatives over the last ten years (See Appendix C).

VI. CONCLUSION AND RECOMMENDATIONS

Latin America and the United States do have defense agreements in place in the form of the Organization of American States and the Rio Treaty, but they are no longer viable for defense of the hemisphere due to conflicting goals and vaguely written rules of operational commitment on the part of the signatories. The decline of the Soviet Union has removed what little threat there was to the area. Even in its prime, Soviet naval deployments (and parallel U.S. naval deployments) to the South Atlantic were few and far between. If the South Atlantic's strategic importance increases due to possible closure of the Suez and Panama Canals in time of hostility, then naval assets should be positioned to protect those areas vice positioning them in the South Atlantic. In peacetime, the South Atlantic is of primary importance for commerce, but of secondary importance strategically.

The possibility of a country within the Western hemisphere coming under massive attack from outside forces is remote at the present time. It is more likely that threats to the hemisphere will either originate within the hemisphere, or will arrive in the form of economic reverberations from some overseas world actor. Threats within the hemisphere include political terrorism, narco-trafficking, narco-terrorism and insurgency. The 1990 Iraqi invasion of Kuwait is an example of extra hemispheric threat which has produced both economic reverberations and balance of power concerns throughout the global community.

These types of threats have been present for a number of years, but have been overshado d to some extent by the cold war. The Rio Treaty was designed for the cold war, and where its utility was questionable for the last forty three years, it now seems obviously inappropriate for these new threats. The 1990 Iraqi invasion of Kuwait provides an example of Latin American threat perception. Several NATO signatories, though they have undergone the same threat reduction problem, mustered some fifty two ships in and around the Persian Gulf in response to the Middle East crisis. Of the Rio Treaty signatories, only Argentina provided two ships for logistical support.[97]

Of the three options mentioned previously; do nothing, revitalize the Rio Treaty, or keep the Treaty and add bilateral agreements, adding bilateral agreements is the best course of action. In order for these bilateral agreements to be worthwhile, the casus foederis must be expanded from the current Rio Treaty definition to include a wider range of threat catalysts. The catalysts should include specific instructions on expected force participation in the event of the following challenges to U.S./Brazilian interests:

---

[97]This observation is not meant to compare NATO and IATRA. Both the NATO signatories and Argentina are acting outside of their respective treaties. Even outside of their treaties however, there is a fundamental difference between NATO and IATRA in threat perception and willingness to commit forces.

•attack on either signatory by any aggressor;
•extra hemispheric threat, either military or economic;
•terrorism or insurgency of any kind; and
•narco-trafficking.

Brazilian naval power projection capabilities and force integration should be enhanced with an emphasis on those capabilities that best complement U.S. Navy capabilities after budget cuts are implemented. Subsidies and incentives to Brazil could include preferred customer status for lend lease and foreign military sales, co-development agreements on future weapons systems, and favorable trading partner status.

Forming a well trained, integrated alliance with a relatively small number of capable navies would provide an alternative to the Rio Treaty. Focused partnerships would be easier to manage, and could be relied upon more than the current weak alliance which pays only lip service to the idea of hemispheric defense. Brazil, with its capability, and historical ties to the United States as a World War II ally is the obvious choice for forming a maritime partnership. Once in place and operating smoothly, other capable and willing countries could be added to the coalition.

Bilateral partnerships should not totally replace the Rio Treaty. The Treaty should be left in place to provide a vehicle for dialogue between countries that are interested. The newly formed bilateral partnerships could assume more of a defense burden by virtue of their increased capability, operability and available incentives.

A bilateral agreement between Brazil and the United States may initially cause tension in countries such as Argentina, particularly if Brazil benefits by increasing its maritime potential. Argentina may request inclusion in such an arrangement, and this could be beneficial to all three countries. It should be noted that Argentina, though it possesses less naval capability than Brazil, sent two ships to the Persian Gulf in support of operation "Desert Storm," where Brazil sent none.

Other problems previously mentioned such as geopolitical considerations and stances on alliances are strictly up to the Brazilians to resolve or negotiate. All the United States can do is present the proposal, be as sensitive to Brazilian concerns as possible and accept the outcome.

Submarines:

Number	Type	Acquired From/Original Name	Weapons
1	Tupi	FRG/(T-209/1400)	Tigerfish Torp
3	Humaita	UK/Oberon	Tigerfish Torp
3	Goias/Bahia	US/Guppy III/II	Tigerfish Torp

Appendix B Continued next page....

Appendix B (continued from previous page)

Principal Surface Combatants:

Mission	Number	Type	Acquir'd From/Original Name	Weapons	Aircraft
Carrier (ASW)	1	Minas Gerais	UK/ Colossus	Airwing	7-8 S-2E, 8 ASH-3H
Destroyer (ASW)	2	Marcilio Dias	US/ Gearing	ASRO, ASTT, 127 mm guns	1 Wasp Helo (Mk 46 Torpedo)
Destroyer (ASW)	5	Mato Grosso	US/ Sumner	ASTT, 127 mm guns	4 with Wasp helo (Mk 46 Torp)
Destroyer	2	Piaui	US/ Fletcher	ASTT, 127 mm, 533 mmTT	none
Frigate (ASW)	4	Niteroi	Brazilian	ASTT, Ikara SUGW, ASW mor, 2 Exocet SSM, 114 mm Gun	1 Lynx Helo
Frigate (GP)	2	Niteroi	Brazilian	Weapons as ASW except 4 Exocet, no Ikara	1 Lynx Helo
Frigate	1	Inhauma	Brazilian	ASRR, 4 Exocet, 114 mm Gun	1 Lynx Helo
Patrol/ Coastal	9	Imperial Marin-heiro PCO	Brazilian		
Patrol/ Coastal	6	Piratini	US/PGM		
Patrol/ Coastal	2	Riverine Patrol			
Mine Warfare	6	Aratu	FRG/ Schutze		
Amphib	1 (600 troop capacity)	Duque de Caxais	US de Soto County)		
Amphib	1 (200 Troop Capacity)	D'Avila	US/LST-511		
Amphib	3 LCU, 3 LCM, 30 LCVP				

Appendix B Continued next page....

Support and Miscellaneous Ships:
1 Marajo AOE, 1 repair ship, 4 tpt, 5 survey/oceanography, 1 mod
Niteroi FF (trg), 5 ocean tugs

Naval Air Force:

ASW: 1 helicopter squadron with 10 ASH-3H

ATTACK: 1 Squadron with 8 Lynx Has 21, 1 with 8 AS-350 (armed),
7 Wasp HAS-, 3 HB-315.

Utility: 1 squadron with 3 AS-332

Training: 1 helo Squadron with 10 TH-57

Air Force Maritime Command:

4 Gp (22 combat aircraft)
ASW afloat: 1 squadron with 12 S-2E
MR/SAR: 4 Squadrons with 14 EMB-110B, 10 EMB-111, 8 UH-1D
armed

Bases

Ocean: Rio de Janeiro (HQ I Naval District, Salvasor (HQ II District),
Natal (HQ III District I, Belem (HQ IV District), Rio Grande (do sul)
(HQ V District) Ladario (HQ VI District)

Riverine: Manaus, Corumba

Source: International Institute for Strategic Studies, *The Military Balance,
1989*, 1990 (Brassey's, 1989) p. 185.

APPENDIX C--JOINT U.S./BRAZILIAN NAVAL INITIATIVES

REGULAR PARTICIPANT IN UNITAS

•Brazilian Phase of UNITAS XXX/89 was first ever quadrilateral phase.   Included U.S./Brazil/Uruguay/Argentina

•Has participated in Phase Zero on many occasions

OTHER OPERATIONS/EXERCISES

•Brazilian navy hosts annual naval control of shipping exercise (Participates in USN Exercises)

•Participant in annual inter-American war game

•USN P-3 Crew to participate in exhange with Brazilian air force

•Brazilian navy participated in FLEETEX 1-89

CARRIER INTERFLEET TRANSFERS

•Participated in PASSEX's with several U.S. Navy aircraft carriers

Appendix C continued next page....

SECURITY ASSISTANCE

•Four Garcia Class Frigates transferred 1989

•Thomaston Class LST Transferred 1989

•SECDEF has approved offer of transfer of four Adams class DDG's (1991-2)

•Brazilan navy has purchased upgraded torpedoes

•May purchase SH-2F's from Kaman

•LOA signed to purchase ex-USNS Sands, hydrographic survey vessel, upon expiration of current lease

AGREEMENTS

•Cooperative project between ONR and Brazilian naval directorate of hydrography and navigation

•Conducting geophysical/oceanographic investigations (ongoing project since 1980)

HIGH LEVEL VISITS

•VADM Nyquist represented SECNAV at Dec 1989 Brazilian Navy Day celebration in Rio marking the arrival of fou. Garcia class frigates

•Several additional visits between high level U.S. Naval officers and their counterparts from BRAZNAV

Appendix C Continued next page . . . .

PERSONNEL EXCHANGES

- Four USN/BRAZNAV officers participating in personnel exchange program
- Naval War College exchange
- Brazilian naval officers attending Naval Postgraduate School, Monterey
- BRAZNAV has liason officer assigned to CINCLANTFLT staff
- USN SEALS periodically attend Brazilian army jungle warfare course
- Foreign exchange and training of midshipmen
- USN Ensign participates in BRAZNAV training cruise

MISCELLANEOUS

- Member of Inter-American naval telecommunications network
- USN mine warfare experts visited Brazilian navy counterparts June 90
- USN experts observed Brazilian navy close-in weapon system currently under development
- CINLANTFLT intelligence exchange

_____

Source: Briefing by Captain Patrick Roth and CDR John G. Karas USN, Western Hemisphere Branch, Politico-Military Policy and Current Plans Division of OP-06, at U.S. Naval Postgraduate School, Monterey, Ca., 9 Sep 1990

BIBLIOGRAPHY

"The Americas at a Crossroads," report of the Inter-American Dialogue, Woodrow Wilson International Center for Scholars, April, 1983.

Atkins, G. Pope, *Latin America in the International Political System.* Boulder: Westview Press, 1989.

Baker, James A., Secretary of State, *Latin America and the U.S.: A New Partnership*, Current Policy Bulletin No. 1160, United States Department of State, Bureau of Public Affairs, Washington D.C.. 30 March 1989

Barton, James D., "The Viability of the Rio Treaty as a Basis for Coalition Defense", paper presented to the National War College, February, 1986.

"Blowup in the Rain Forest", *Time*, April 90.

Bonturi, Orlando, *Brazil and the Vital South Atlantic*, National Defense University Press, 1988.

Branco, Robert J., *The United States and Brazil.* Washington D.C.: National Defense University Press, 1984.

Brazil: A Country Study, United States Government as represented by the Secretary of the Army, 1983.

Breemer, Jan S., "The Soviet Navy's SSBN Bastions: New Questions Raised", *RUSI Journal of the Royal United Services Institute for Defence Studies*, June 1987.

Bush, George Herbert Walker, *National Security Strategy of the United States.* The White House, March 1990.

Child, Jack, *Geopolitics and Conflict in South America.* New York: Praeger, 1985.

Child, John, *Unequal Alliance; The Inter American Military System, 1938-1978*. Boulder: Westview Press. 1980.

Chief of Naval Operations, *The Maritime Strategy*. OPNAV 60 P-1-89, Department of the Navy, Revision 4, 23 February 1989.

Daily, John L., "If Mikhail Muddles Through", *U.S. Naval Institute Proceedings*, June 1990.

"Direction of Trade Statistics Yearbook", International Monetary Fund, Publication Services, Washington, D.C., 1990.

Dougherty, James E. and Pfaltzgraff, Robert L *Contending Theories of International Relations*, New York: Harper and Row Publishers, 1981.

Executive News Services. APn 04/17 2213. Brazil-Nuclear. The Associated Press, 1990.

Gray, Colin, "Tomorrow's Forecast: Warmer/Still Cloudy". *U.S. Naval Institute Proceedings*, May 1990.

Hayes, Margaret Daly, *Latin America and the U.S. National Interest*, Boulder: Westview Press, 1984.

Holsti, K. J., *International Politics, A Framework for Analysis*, Englewood Cliffs: Prentice Hall, 1988.

International Institute for Strategic Studies. *The Military Balance, 1989-1990* Brassey's, 1989.

Kelly, Philip and Child, Jack, eds *Geopolitics of the Southern Cone and Antarctica* Boulder and London: Lynne Rienner Publishers, 1988.

Lamb, Christina, "Brazil will 'partially lift' Moratorium", *Financial Times of London*, December 19, 1990.

"Collor Address on Treaty With Argentina," (in Portuguese), *Folha de Sao Paulo*, 29 Nov 90, p. A 3, translated and reported in FIBIS LAT-90-236, 7 December 1990.

Lamb, Christopher, "The Nature of Proxy Warfare", in *The Future of Conflict in the 1980s,* eds. William J. Taylor, Jr. and Steven A. Maaranen Washington, D.C.: Center for Strategic and International Studies, 1982.

Lenczowski, George, *The Middle East in World Affairs*, Ithaca and London: Cornell University Press, 1980.

Liska, George F., *Nations in Alliance*, Baltimore: The Johns Hopkins Press, 1968.

Lowenthal, Abraham, "Rethinking US Interests in the Western Hemisphere", *Journal of Interamerican Studies and World Affairs* , vol 29, Spring 1987.

Luria, Rene, "The Brazilian Armed Forces Budgets and Ambition Diverge", *International Defense Review*, July 1989.

Molineu, Harold, *U.S. Policy Toward Latin America.* Boulder: Westview Press, 1986.

Morrocco, John D., "New Pentagon Strategy Shifts Focus From Europe to Regional Conflicts". *Aviation Week and Space Technology*, 13 August 90.

Morris, Michael A., *Expansion of Third World Navies.* London: MacMillan Press, 1987.

Murcio, Javier F., and Rosales, Roberto, *World Markets Report.* Lexington: DRI/McGraw-Hill, 1990.

Nuechterlein, Donald E. *America Overcommitted.* Lexington: The University Press of Kentucky, 1985.

North, David M., "Aerospace Officials Praise Performance of CBA-123". *Aviation Week and Space Technology*, September 10, 1990.

Oladimeji, Olutunde A. Captain, "Nigeria: On Becoming a Sea Power". *U.S. Naval Institute Proceedings*, March 89.

O'Rourke, Gerald G., U.S. Navy (Retired), "Our Peaceful Navy", *U.S. Naval Institute Proceedings*, April 1989.

Pesce, Eduardo Italo, "Brazil's Silent Service", *U.S. Naval Institute Proceedings*, March 1989.

Powell, Colin, General USA, "Crystal Balls Don't Always Help". *U.S. Naval Institute Proceedings*, May 90.

Rosenfeld, Stephen S., "By Latins for Latins", *The Washington Post*, 17 January 86.

Russell, Roberto, "Argentina: Ten Years of Foreign Policy Toward the Southern Cone", in *Geopolitics of the Southern Cone and Antarctica*, eds. Philip Kelly and Jack Child, Boulder: Lynne Rienner Publishers, 1988.

Sabrosky, Alan Ned, ed. *Alliances in U.S. Foreign Policy*, Boulder: Westview Press, 1988.

Scheina, Robert L. "Latin American Navies", *U.S. Naval Institute Proceedings*, March 90.

Scheina, Robert L. *Latin America, a Naval History 1810-1987*. Annapolis: Naval Institute Press, 1987.

Selcher, Wayne A. "Brazilian-Argentine Relations in the 1980s; From Wary Rivalry to Friendly Competition". *Journal of Interamerican Studies and World Affairs.* Summer 1985.

Selcher, Wayne A., "Brazil and the Southern Cone Subsystem" in *South America into the 1990s. ed. G. Pope Atkins.* Boulder: Westview Press, 1990.

Stella, Joaquin, Captain, "Stabilizing the Uneasy Atlantic". *U.S. Naval Institute Proceedings*, March 89.

Tollefson, Scott D. "Brazil, the United States, and the Missile Technology Control Regime". NPS-56-90-006, paper prepared for the Naval Postgraduate School, Monterey, Ca., March 1990.

Tritten, James J., "America Promises to Come Back: A New National Strategy", NPS-NS-91-003, Naval Postgraduate School, Monterey, Ca., 26 December 1990.

Trost, Carlisle A. H., Admiral USN, "Maritime Strategy for the 1990's". *U.S. Naval Institute Proceedings*, May 1990.

Vaky, Viron P. et al., *Governence in the Western Hemisphere* . New York: Praeger, 1983.

Wesson, Robert, *The Latin American Military Institution* New York: Praeger, 1986.

Wirth, John D., et al., eds. *State and Society in Brazil.* Boulder and London: Westview Press, 1987.

Wolf, Charles Jr., Watkins, Katherine, *Developing Cooperative Forces in the Third World: Report of a Rand Conference, March 14-15 1985*, prepared for the Office of the Under Secretary of Defense for Policy, Santa Monica: Rand, 1985.

World Military Expenditures and Arms Transfers 1971-1980, United States Arms Control and Disarmament Agency, Washington D.C.: U.S. Government Printing Office, 1983.

World Military Expenditures and Arms Tra⋅ ⋅s 1989, United States Arms Control and Disarmament Agency, Washington D.C.: U.S. Government Printing Office, 1990.